Planning for Learning through Numbers

by Jenni Clarke Illustrated by Cathy Hughes

Contents

2-3 Making plans

4-7 Using the Early Learning Goals

8-9 Week 1: Number Hunt

10-11 Week 2: Musical Numbers

12-13 Week 3: Cooking with Numbers

14-15 Week 4: Arty Numbers

16-17 Week 5: Shopping with Numbers

18-19 Week 6: We Love Numbers

20 Bringing it all together - 'We love Numbers'

21 Resources

22 Collecting evidence of children's learning

23 Skills overview of six-week plan

24 Home links

Inside back cover Parent's Page

Published by Practical Pre-School Books
St Jude's Church, Dulwich Road, Herne Hill, London, SE24 0PB Tel. 020 7738 5454
© MA Education 2010
www.practicalpreschoolbooks.com
Front cover image © iStockphoto.com/Marilyn Nieves. Back cover image © iStockphoto.com/Alessandro Contadini
All rights reserved. No part of this publication may be reproduced, stored in a retrieval system, or transmitted by any means, electronic, mechanical, photocopied or otherwise, without the prior permission of the publisher.
Planning for Learning through Numbers ISBN: 978 1 90724 101 7

Making plans

The purpose of planning is to make sure that all children enjoy a broad and balanced curriculum. All planning should be useful. Plans are working documents which you spend time preparing, but which should later repay your efforts. Try to be concise. This will help you in finding information quickly when you need it.

Long Term Plans

Preparing a long-term plan, which maps out the curriculum during a year or even two, will help you to ensure that you are providing a variety of activities and are meeting the requirements of the Statutory Framework for the Early Years Foundation Stage (2007).

Your long-term plans need not be detailed. Divide the time period over which you are planning into fairly equal sections, such as half terms. Choose a topic for each section. Young children benefit from making links between the new ideas they encounter so as you select each topic, think about the time of year in which you plan to do it. A topic about minibeasts will not be very successful in November!

Although each topic will address all the areas of learning, some could focus on a specific area. For example, a topic on shapes lends itself well to activities relating to mathematics. Another topic might particularly encourage the appreciation of stories. Try to make sure that you provide a variety of topics in your long-term plans, such as:

Autumn 1	Nursery Rhymes
Autumn 2	Toys/Christmas
Spring 1	Weather
Spring 2	Minibeasts
Summer 3	Numbers
Summer 4	Farms

Medium-term plans will outline the contents of a topic in a little more detail. One way to start this process is by brainstorming on a large piece of paper. Work with your team writing down all the activities you can think of which are relevant to the topic. As you do this it may become clear that some activities go well together.

Think about dividing them into themes. The topic of Numbers, for example, has themes such as Musical Numbers, Arty Numbers, Cooking with Numbers. At this stage it is helpful to make a chart. Write the theme ideas down the side of the chart and put a different area of learning at the top of each column. Now you can insert your brainstormed ideas and quickly see where there are gaps. As you complete the chart take account of children's earlier experiences and provide opportunities for them to progress.

Refer back to the Statutory Framework for the Early Years Foundation Stage and check that you have addressed as many different aspects as you can. Once all your medium-term plans are complete make sure that there are no neglected areas.

Day to Day Plans

The plans you make for each day will outline aspects such as:

- resources needed;
- the way in which you might introduce activities;
- safety;
- the organisation of adult help;

Making plans

- size of the group;
- timing;
- key vocabulary;
- individual needs.

Identify the learning and ELGs which each activity is intended to promote. Make a note of any assessments or observations that you are likely to carry out. After using the plans, make notes of which activities were particularly successful, or any changes you would make another time

A Final Note

Planning should be seen as flexible. Not all groups meet every day, and. not all children attend every day. Any part of the plan can be used independently, stretched over a longer period or condensed to meet the needs of any group. You will almost certainly adapt the activities as children respond to them in different ways and bring their own ideas, interests and enthusiasms. Be prepared to be flexible over timing as some ideas prove more popular than others. The important thing is to ensure that the children are provided with a varied and enjoyable curriculum which meets their individual developing needs.

- Find out on page 20 how the topic can be brought together in a grand finale involving parents, children and friends.
- There is additional material to support the working partnership of families and children in the form of a 'Home links' page, and a photocopiable 'Parent's page' found at the back of the book.

It is important to appreciate that the ideas presented in this book will only be a part of your planning. Many activities which will be taking place as routine in your group may not be mentioned. For example, it is assumed that sand, dough, water, puzzles, floor toys and large scale apparatus are part of the ongoing pre-school experience, as are the opportunities to develop ICT skills. Role play areas, stories, rhymes and singing, and group discussion times are similarly assumed to be happening each week although they may not be a focus for described activities. Groups should also ensure that there is a balance of adult-led and child-initiated activities

Using the Book

- Collect or prepare suggested resources as listed on page 21.
- Read the section which outlines links to the Early Learning Goals (pages 4-7) and explains the rationale for the topic of Number
- For each weekly theme two activities are described in detail as an example to help you in your planning and preparation. Key vocabulary, questions and learning opportunities are identified.
- The skills chart on page 23 will help you to see at a glance which aspects of children's development are being addressed as a focus each week.
- As children take part in the Number topic activities, their learning will progress. 'Collecting evidence' on page 22 explains how you might monitor children's achievements.

Using this book in Northern Ireland, Scotland and Wales

Although the curriculum guidelines in Northern Ireland, Scotland and Wales differ, the activities in this book are still appropriate for use throughout the United Kingdom. They are designed to promote the development of early skills and to represent good practice in the early years

Glossary

EYFS: Early Years Foundation Stage
ELG: Early Learning Goal

Using the 'Early Learning Goals'

Having decided on your topic and made your medium-term plans you can use the Early Learning Goals to highlight the key learning opportunities your activities will address. The Early Learning Goals are split into six areas: Personal, Social and Emotional Development, Communication, Language and Literacy, Problem Solving, Reasoning and Numeracy, Knowledge and Understanding of the World, Physical Development and Creative Development. Do not expect each of your topics to cover every goal but your long-term plans should allow for each child to work towards all of the goals

The following section lists the Early Learning Goals in point form to show what children are expected to be able to do in each area of learning by the time they enter Year 1. These points will be used throughout this book to show how activities for a topic on numbers link to these expectations. For example, Personal. Social and Emotional Development point 9 is 'understand what is wrong, what is right and why'. Activities suggested which provide the opportunity for children to do this will have the reference PS9. This will enable you to see which parts of the Early Learning Goals are covered in a given week and plan for areas to be revisited and developed.

In addition you can ensure that activities offer variety in the outcomes to be encountered. Often a similar activity may be carried out to achieve different outcomes. For example, during this topic children make different salt dough loaves for the bakers van. They will be learning about bread, experimenting with dough, expressing themselves creatively as they design their loaves, extending their vocabulary and working as part of a group as well as counting and measuring ingredients. It is important therefore that activities have clearly defined learning outcomes so that these may be emphasised during the activity and for recording purposes.

Personal, Social and Emotional Development (PS)

This area of learning incorporates attitudes, skills and understanding and is a pre-condition for children's success in all other learning. The goals include children's personal, social/emotional, moral and spiritual development and the establishment of good attitudes to their learning.

By the end of the EYFS children should:

PS1   Continue to be interested, excited and motivated to learn.
PS2   Be confident to try new activities, initiate ideas and speak in a familiar group.
PS3   Maintain attention, concentrate and sit quietly when appropriate.
PS4   Respond to significant experiences showing a range of feelings when appropriate.
PS5   Have a developing awareness of their own needs, views and feelings, and be sensitive to the needs, views and feelings of others.
PS6   Have a developing respect for their own cultures and beliefs and those of other people.
PS7   Form good relationships with adults and peers.
PS8   Work as a part of a group or class taking turns and sharing fairly, understanding that there needs to be agreed values and codes of behaviour for groups of people, including adults and children, to work together harmoniously.
PS9   Understand what is right, what is wrong and why.
PS10   Consider the consequences of their words and actions for themselves and others.

PS11 Dress and undress independently and manage their own personal hygiene.
PS12 Select and use activities and resources independently.
PS13 Understand that people have different needs, views, cultures and beliefs which need to be treated with respect.
PS14 Understand that they can expect others to treat their needs, views, cultures and beliefs with respect.

During the topic of numbers children will work together on several collaborative activities. They will develop skills of listening to each other and taking turns as ideas are shared and preferences expressed. As they share toys and equipment children will learn to think about each others' needs and feelings. Many of the areas outlined above, though, will be covered on an almost incidental basis as children carry out the activities described in this book for the other areas of learning. During undirected free choice times they will be developing independence (PS12) whilst any small group activity which involves working with an adult will help children to build effective relationships (PS7).

Communication, Language and Literacy (L)

By the end of the EYFS children should:

L1 Interact with others, negotiating plans and activities and taking turns in conversation.
L2 Enjoy listening to and using spoken and written language, and readily turn to it in their play and learning.
L3 Sustain attentive listening, responding to what they have heard by relevant comments, questions or actions.
L4 Listen with enjoyment, and respond to stories, songs and other music, rhymes and poems and make up their own stories, songs, rhymes and poems.
L5 Extend their vocabulary, exploring the meaning and sounds of new words.
L6 Speak clearly and audibly with confidence and control and show awareness of the listener.
L7 Use language to imagine and recreate roles and experiences.
L8 Use talk to organise, sequence and clarify thinking, ideas, feelings and events.
L9 Hear and say sounds in words in the order in which they occur.
L10 Link sounds to letters, naming and sounding the letters of the alphabet.
L11 Use their phonic knowledge to write simple regular words and make phonetically plausible attempts at more complex words.
L12 Explore and experiment with sounds, words and texts.
L13 Retell narratives in the correct sequence, drawing on language patterns of stories.
L14 Read a range of familiar and common words and simple sentences independently.
L15 Show an understanding of the elements of stories such as main character, sequence of events and openings, and how information can be found in non-fiction texts to answer questions about where, who, why and how.
L16 Know that print carries meaning and, in English, is read from left to right and top to bottom.
L17 Attempt writing for different purposes, using features of different forms such as lists, stories and instructions.
L18 Write their own names and other things such as labels and captions, and begin to form simple sentences, sometimes using punctuation.
L19 Use a pencil and hold it effectively to form recognisable letters, most of which are correctly formed.

The activities suggested for the theme of numbers include some which are based on quality picture books and stories. They allow children to enjoy listening to the books and to respond in a variety of ways to what they hear, reinforcing and extending their vocabularies. Throughout the topic opportunities are described in which children are encouraged to explore the sounds of words, to use descriptive vocabulary and to see some of their ideas recorded in both pictures and words.

Problem Solving, Reasoning and Numeracy (N)

By the end of the EYFS children should:

N1   Say and use number names in order in familiar contexts.
N2   Count reliably up to ten everyday objects.
N3   Recognise numerals 1 to 9.
N4   Use developing mathematical ideas and methods to solve practical problems.
N5   In practical activities and discussion, begin to use the vocabulary involved in adding and subtracting.
N6   Use language such as 'more' or 'less' to compare two numbers.
N7   Find one more or one less than a number from one to ten.
N8   Begin to relate addition to combining two groups of objects and subtraction to 'taking away'.
N9   Use language such as 'greater', 'smaller', 'heavier', or lighter' to compare quantities
N10 Talk about, recognise and recreate simple patterns.
N11 Use language such as 'circle' or 'bigger' to describe the shape and size of solids and flat shapes.
N12 Use everyday words to describe position.

The theme of numbers provides a meaningful context for problem solving, reasoning and numeracy. A number of activities allow children to develop mathematical language and early understandings of number names. Children are encouraged to use numbers in their everyday play as well as developing measuring skills and shape recognition.

Knowledge and Understanding of the World (K)

By the end of the EYFS children should:

K1   Investigate objects and materials by using all of their senses as appropriate.
K2   Find out about, and identify, some features of, living things, objects and events they observe.
K3   Look closely at similarities, differences, patterns and change.
K4   Ask questions about why things happen and how things work.
K5   Build and construct with a wide range of objects, selecting appropriate resources and adapting their work where necessary.
K6   Select tools and techniques they need to shape, assemble and join the materials they are using.
K7   Find out about and identify the uses of everyday technology and use communication technology and programmable toys to support their learning.
K8   Find out about past and present events in their own lives, and in those of their families and other people they know.
K9   Observe, find out about and identify features in the place they live and the natural world.
K10 Find out about their environment and talk about those features they like and dislike.
K11 Begin to know about their own cultures and beliefs and those of other people.

The topic of numbers offers many opportunities for children to explore and investigate, to make observations and to ask questions. They can extend their awareness of the local environment as they search for numbers and record their findings. They will learn more about the use of number in everyday life, and begin to develop appropriate vocabulary and understanding as they explain their reasoning and observations.

Physical Development (PD)

By the end of the EYFS children should:

PD1 Move with confidence, imagination and in safety.
PD2 Move with control and co-ordination.
PD3 Travel around, under, over and through balancing and climbing equipment.

PD4 Show awareness of space, of themselves and of others.
PD5 Recognise the importance of keeping healthy and those things which contribute to this.
PD6 Recognise the changes that happen to their bodies when they are active.
PD7 Use a range of small and large equipment.
PD8 Handle tools, objects, construction and malleable materials safely and with increasing control.

Through the theme of numbers children will have opportunities to develop the skills of moving with confidence and imagination. Activities such as creating artwork and resources for their play will offer experiences of working with tools and materials in a practical and purposeful context. There are many opportunities for developing confidence and control of movement as they play number based games and for children to become aware of what happens to their bodies when they are active.

Creative Development (C)

By the end of the EYFS children should:

C1 Respond in a variety of ways to what they see, hear, smell, touch and feel.
C2 Express and communicate their ideas, thoughts and feelings by using a widening range of materials, suitable tools, imaginative and role play, movement, designing and making, and a variety of songs and musical instruments.
C3 Explore colour, texture, shape, form and space in two or three dimensions.
C4 Recognise and explore how sounds can be changed, sing simple songs from memory, recognise repeated sounds and sound patterns and match movements to music.
C5 Use their imagination in art and design, music, dance, imaginative and role-play and stories.

During this topic children will experience working with a variety of materials as they print and paint, make models, and explore a range of creative making tasks. Music is used as a way of supporting imaginative movement, with suggestions for the use of pattern in pitch and tempo. Throughout all the activities children are encouraged to talk about what they see and feel as they communicate their ideas in 2D and 3D work, dance, music and role-play.

Week 1
Number Hunt

Personal, Social and Emotional Development
- Begin with a number hunt, either in the room, immediate vicinity or on a walk around the area. This can be done with small groups, which then means the children can discuss different things they saw and compare numbers. Discuss how to record what they see, maybe adults writing numbers on a clipboard, talking into a Dictaphone, children taking photos with a digital camera, children with a list of numbers that they tally mark against. This will set the focus for the 6 weeks, encouraging children to be more aware of numbers in everyday life. Ensure that the children are aware of the safety rules for walking around the environment before you leave the room, or how they need to think about others if they are hunting inside the room, some children may be playing a quiet game. (PS3, 4, 7, 9)
- Make a number trail (see activity opposite). (PS1, 2, 8, 10)

Communication, Language and Literacy
- Sit outside and share a variety of number based books such as *Kipper's Book of Numbers* and *One Smiling Sister*. Children can make their own book of numbers either individually, with a friend or in a small group, based on that they found on the hunt or can find in the outside area. (L2, 3, 4, 18)
- Read the non-fiction book *How many Baby Pandas?*. This links information with counting and is best shared with a few children at a time so that they can count the pandas as you read. Being in a small group allows them to discuss what is happening on the pages and talk about the problems facing pandas in the wild. (L3, 5, 8, 15, 16)

Problem Solving, Reasoning and Numeracy
- Add number cutters and small beads or candleholders to the dough box resources. Observe the play and when an interest is shown in the number cutters encourage the children to have a go at making numbers, encourage them to feel around the number shapes with their eyes open and then with their eyes closed, can they guess which number it is? Can they push one bead or candle holder into the number 1? What about number 2, how many beads do you need? (N1, 2, 3, 4)
- Go for a short walk and look at the number plates of vehicles, talk about why vehicles have numbers and how it may be good to have number plates on the vehicles at the setting. The children can then be encourage to take resources outside to the vehicles and make number plates for each one. Lots of problem solving to be done. (N3, 4)

Knowledge and Understanding of the World
- Build a street (see activity opposite). (K5, 6, 9)
- Add a basket full of paired socks to the outdoor washing line resources, ensuing that there is a variety of sizes, texture and patterns. Observe the play that evolves from these resources and encourage the children to notice that there are always 2 socks in a pair. Can they find two the same? Can they sort and match pairs for size, patterns, texture and colour, counting how many pairs are red for example. Discuss who the owners of the socks might be, a giant or a mouse? Make links with home by asking if anyone has socks like this pair at home? What else do you usually have as a pair? (K1, 2, 3)

Physical Development
Both the following ideas are based outside where there is more space, especially if lots of children are involved.
- Physical number games with a small group or everyone such as calling out a number and an action '1 stamp', '2 jump' etc, for more able children hold up number cards and for older children ask them to make up simple sequences with actions and numbers, they could even record these for others to try. (PD1, 4)
- Find someone with the same number game. Each child is given a card with either a number of objects or a numeral on it, they keep it a secret, when everyone has a card and is happy with their number they move about the space saying their number, when they find someone with the same they stand still together until everyone is in number groups. Each group in turn chooses an action and does that action their number of times, the other groups count and call out the number.

For older children the numbers may all be even or odd, do they notice? (PD1, 2, 4)

Creative Development

- Make birthday cards for some toys, each toy has a label to show their age. Look at and discuss a range of birthday cards, looking at the numbers on the outside and inside of the cards. Ensure there is a range of resources available for making the cards and for creating the numbers such as stencils, cards to cut up, numbers to trace around or number stamps. (C2, 3)
- Add laminated numbers and blu-tack (or equivalent) to the resources in the construction area (both outdoors and indoors) Encourage the children to use the numbers on their buildings, perhaps to show which garage is for which car, how many blocks high a tower is, how many goats can fit on the bridge etc. (C2, 3)

Activity: Number Trail

Learning opportunity: Counting numbers in sequence from 1–10.

Early Learning Goal: Problem Solving, Reasoning and Numeracy. Count reliably up to 10 everyday objects. Recognise numerals 1–9.

Resources: Pictures, numerals, collections of objects, boxes, baskets, pegs and bags.

Key Vocabulary: Number names, next, start, finish.

Organisation: Small groups.

What to do: Discuss and design a number trail with a small group of children who you have observed are interested in numbers or treasure hunts. They can then lay the trail for other children to discover, the trail could be pictures, numerals or objects from 1-10. The hunters need to find the numbers in the correct order, maybe as a group or as individuals. You could encourage them to shout or jump or clap the number when they find it. Ensure that the trail is set at the appropriate level for the children. For older children there could be a box of an object under each number and they can count the right number of each objects into their bag. They can then compare their objects with a friend's objects; do they have the same amount? What happens if they put their collections together?

If the children continue to make number trails in their independent learning time, encourage them to develop their learning by adding timers and recording materials.

Activity: Make a street

Learning opportunity: Recognising and using numbers in order for a purpose while creating a small world scene.

Early Learning Goal: Knowledge and Understanding of the World. Build and construct with a wide range of objects, selecting appropriate resources and adapting their work where necessary.

Resources: A variety of boxes, creative tools and materials, toy cars and people, sticky labels and mark making materials, sticky number labels for those who need them, a large board or piece of paper.

Key Vocabulary: Next to, beside, in front, behind, odd, even.

Organisation: Small groups.

What to do: Look at photos taken on the walk and pictures of street scenes. Discuss the house numbers and how they increase by one or two, often the numbers on one side of the street are even numbers and on the other side odd. Put number tiles in the same order.

Read a letter from a group of toy people asking for a new street to live in, encourage the children to choose their resources carefully, talk about garages or parking spaces for the cars next to, in front of the houses or as a group near the houses, how will they know which is their garage?

When the houses have been made and a road drawn large enough for the cars to travel on how do we know which house to place where? The children can decide how the numbers in the street are going to work, and then position their houses. The street will also need a name.

These streets can then be used in child initiated play and extended by some challenges - perhaps the postman has a bag of letters to be delivered or the milkman a list of which houses want milk, can the children help?

Display

Make a grand collage of numbers seen everyday– house numbers, car numbers, cereal packets, birthday cards, phones, recipes, bus numbers, speed signs, clocks. In front of this on a table place the toys and birthday cards that the children have made, can the children give each toy the correct card? Add some baked dough birthday cakes and numbered biscuits to extend and continue the interest as the week continues.

Week 2
Musical Numbers

Personal, Social and Emotional Development
- Pass the sound - Sit with a small group of children and pass sounds around the circle: adult makes a sound, child on left/right repeats sound, next child repeats the sound until it gets back to the adult. The children can take turns to start a sound round when they understand the game. You can use vocal sounds or an instrument. Vary how many times a sound is made for example 'peep, peep' or tap a tambourine 3 times. For older children mix sounds up, 'la pop, la pop'. This can be played inside or outside. (P3, 8)
- Make a set of small world number rhyme shoeboxes with the children for them to be able to choose to take home and share with their parents. Rhymes such as five little ducks went swimming one day…five little aliens…five speckled frogs. The box will need simple scenery, characters from the rhyme, some number tiles and the number rhyme on a card. The shoebox can be adapted so that the short end opens, this enables you to create simple scenery for the rhyme action to take place in, or add some material to the box for a pond, space etc. These boxes could also be available for child-initiated play. (P1, 2, 7)

Communication, Language and Literacy
- Talk about favourite rhymes and songs, sing them, tape them, type them up and decorate them and display them. They can be laminated and hung outside on a 'rhyme tree' for the children to access when they want. The cards could be kept in a special box and randomly picked out for waiting or transition times such as tidy up time or home time. (L2, 4, 6, 14, 15)
- Act out number rhymes such as five specked frogs outside where there is space to jump off the 'log' into the 'pond', or space to fly off in a flying saucer. Adapt the number depending on the size of the group of children. Encourage them to reverse the action too, by jumping back out of the pond onto the log. You can use a giant dice to decide how many jump off or on. Older children can be challenged to record what is happening and be involved in addition and subtraction. (L1, 2, 3, 4, 7, 8)

Problem Solving, Reasoning and Numeracy
- Musical numbers game – see activity opposite. (N2, 3, 4)
- Go outside with a basket of interesting percussion instruments, (ensure the children have time to explore these in independent learning,) talk about the sounds the instruments make whether they are long or short sounds, loud or quiet. Give each instrument type a number sticker up to 9. They can choose 2 or 3 instruments each. Hold up a number or roll a dice: can they play the instrument with the same number and stop when the number card is turned over or the dice picked up? These resources can be accessible for the children to play independently or teach to their friends. (N1, 2, 3)

Knowledge and Understanding of the World
- Go outside with a small group of children and talk about all the things they can see, discuss what they like and why, then make up a song, for example 'I see one bench to sit on, I see two trees to play under, I see…' These songs can be recorded and shared with other children. To encourage them to make up their own in child initiated learning time have hand held tape recorders available. (K2, 4, 9)
- Make a noisy number board. Draw large numbers on a board and invite the children to cover them with materials that will make a sound for example scrunchy cellophane, rigged cardboard and a wooden stick, bubble wrap, beads to clack together or bells to jingle. Encourage the children to experiment and discover sounds as well as using skills for attaching materials to the board. (K1, 5, 6)

Physical Development
- Play finger action rhymes that include numbers such as ;
  Five Fat Peas:
  Five fat peas in a pea pod pressed
  (*children hold hand in a fist*)
  One grew, two grew, so did all the rest.
  (*put thumb and fingers up one by one*)
  They grew and grew
  (*raise hand in the air very slowly*)
  And did not stop,

Until one day
The pod went POP!
(*children clap hands together*)

- Five Fat Sausages Sizzling in a Pan and 5 Little Ducks went swimming one day (using sign language with these rhymes is good fun. Use the Makaton Nursery Rhymes Video [VHS] Dave Benson) (PD 1, 2, 4)
- Read and act out *Bearobics: A Hip-Hop Counting Story* with a large group of children. This is great to do outside (in the jungle!) The children can wear animal hats with a number if there are too many children have 2 or 3 of a type, add some rhythmic music and it's a good physical workout! Discuss what is happening to their bodies when they jump and dance around. (PD 1, 2, 4, 6)

Creative Development

- See Activity Finger rhyme gloves (C1, 2, 5)
- Make some colourful shakers out of containers or tubes, dried beans or lentils. Try to count how many lentils, talk about hundreds and thousands, large numbers fascinate young children. Encourage the children to decorate the shakers with patterns and pictures, when each one is finished put a sticker on with a number, they can choose which number. These can then be used for music and number recognition games. (C2, 3, 4, 5)

Activity: Musical numbers

Learning opportunity: Number recognition and counting while playing a game.

Early Learning Goal: Problem Solving, Reasoning and Numeracy. Recognise numbers 1-9

Resources: Lively music and a player for outside, several sets of 1-9 laminated large number cards, puppet, washing line, pegs.

Key Vocabulary: Number names 1-9

Organisation: Small group

What to do: Go outside where there is space for moving without disturbing others. Place number cards around the space, these may have pictures or dots to help children recognise the numeral. Play the music and the children dance, when the music stops they either pick up any number and then try to call them out in order or hang them on the washing line, or look for a specific number such as the same number as the puppet is holding, (or one more, one less for older children).

Ensure the children know where the resources are for playing the game in child initiated learning time.

Activity: Finger rhyme gloves

Learning opportunity: Working imaginatively to create simple resources for a game.

Early Learning Goal: Creative Development. Use their imagination in art and design, music, dance, imaginative and role-play and stories.

Resources: Easily put on gloves, velcro circles, card, creative materials, books and pictures of sea shore creatures, a rhyme such as

> 'One baby turtle alone and new.
> Finds a friend, and then there are two.
> Two baby turtles crawl down to the sea.
> They find another, and then there are three.
> Three baby turtles crawl along the shore.
> They find another, and then there are four.
> Four baby turtles go for a dive.
> Up swims another, and then there are five.'

Key Vocabulary: How many, one more, one less, one, two, three, four, five

Organisation: Small group

What to do: Share the rhyme and show the children a glove with 5 Velcro spots and 5 animal pictures that can be added or removed. Let them play with the glove and the rhyme. Look in the books and at the pictures and say the rhyme using different animals. Ask the children to draw their own pictures and make their own rhyme glove. Remember it does not have to look like a baby seal to be one! Try out the rhymes and the gloves. Older children could be encouraged to work the rhyme backwards too.

These gloves can then be shown to other children, but be ready this may generate more glove making in child independent learning time, so have plenty of resources ready!

Display

Place the musical number board where children and visitors can experiment with it. Put the shakers on a table in front as they are made, can they be put in numerical order? Can older children 'write' some music for others to try playing?

Week 3
Cooking with numbers

Personal, Social and Emotional Development
- Activity Fruit Salad (PS1, 2, 5, 7)
- Organise a set of picnic resources in a basket with some teddies and a note saying that they would like help with setting out their picnic. Leave for the children to find in child initiated learning session. Observe the play, join in if invited and help to count out the plates etc. For older children make sure that there are not enough for all the bears to have 1 each of something so that problem solving occurs. (PS8, 9, 12, 13)

Communication, Language and Literacy
- Read the book 'From the Garden: A Counting Book about Growing Food'. Use props such as pictures of food on sticks planted in the soil, toy food, baskets, wheelbarrows and spades to collect the vegetables from the garden as the story is read. Encourage the children to retell the story using the props and to talk about what they grow at home or at the setting. (L2, 3, 4, 7)
- Look through the recipe books in the book corner together, talk about what they eat at home, like, dislike, favourites. Point out amounts, weights and numbers that are used in the recipes for ingredients and oven temperature and timing. You could make a 'my favourite meal' plate with the children by making food from recycled material and sticking it on a paper plate. These can be displayed for comments and discussion (L1, 3, 5, 8)

Problem Solving, Reasoning and Numeracy
- Place a variety of scales, balances, measuring jugs, spoons and baking containers into the home corner/kitchen play area with labelled containers of ingredients such as dried beans, lentils, rice and pasta as well as 'tins' of food that do not open, coloured rice and tiny pieces of paper are good for seasonings! Make some simple recipe cards using grams, mls and spoonfuls and observe the play, enhancing learning with modelling, conversation and open-ended questions. 'Something smells nice' is a great comment to use to get involved in the play in a natural way, followed up by 'what have you added to make it smell so tasty?' Be prepared for a long stay in the play kitchen and don't forget to help with the washing up! (N2, 3, 5, 6)
- Have a variety of 'how to build cards' in the outside construction area, such as number of bricks of a certain shape needed to build a tower or a ' cement' recipe with some small lightweight bricks, so they can count, measure and build. Encourage older children to make their own 'how to' cards or experiment to get the perfect 'cement'. (N1, 2, 3, 4, 5, 6, 9, 12)

Knowledge and Understanding of the World
- Put compost instead of sand in the sand tray outside with cake cases, sieves, spoons, cake trays, jugs etc With a small group encourage them to fill up the cases or tins, how many spoonfuls are needed, do they need to add water, if so how much? The resources can be left for other children to access in child independent learning time. (K1, 4, 6)
- A small group of children can prepare a snack each day from a different country such as French Toast (bread dipped in egg and milk then fried), Small Italian Pizzas, Mexican Tortilla Buñuelos (Tortillas spread with cinnamon and sugar, rolled up tight and baked for 5 minutes in the oven), German Breakfast (Muesli with fresh fruit), American smoothies (Yoghurt, fruit and fruit juice blended together) Write out the recipe with pictures so it is simple to follow, eg 1 small spoonful of cinnamon. (K1, 4, 6, 11)

Physical Development
- Activity Making Witch/Wizard Stew (PD1, 7, 8)
- Look at pictures of bread delivery vans with a few children, talk about how to turn the tractor and trailer into bread delivery van, plan, design, make and decorate the 'van'. Talk about bread and how it is healthy and needs to be fresh to the shops everyday. Discuss how the driver will know what bread to deliver where and make appropriate forms. Help the children to act out the roles of van driver, shopkeeper and bakery. (PD4, 5, 7, 8)

Creative Development
- Make Iced Number biscuits using a basic biscuit recipe and number shaped cutters. Help them

make coloured icing for the top and add chopped, dried or fresh fruit for extra counting. Enjoy counting, recognising and eating the numbers! Older children could record what is put on which number biscuit and how popular that topping is for future cooking sessions. (C1, 3, 5)

- Have a variety of different breads for the children to cut, explore and taste, talk about the different grains and seeds used. You could make some real bread dough and rolls with the children as well as making salt dough to make different loaves and rolls out for the baker's van. Paint the hardened dough and varnish with PVA glue for a longer life! (C1, 2, 3, 5)

Activity: Making Witch/Wizard Stew

Learning opportunity: Developing physical skills while counting, creating and playing with natural resources outside.

Early Learning Goal: Move with confidence, imagination and in safety.

Resources: Large cauldron type pot(s), recipe cards with natural ingredients such as 1 cup of water, 2 daisy petals, 3 blades of grass (ensure there are pictures alongside the words), the magic chant on a card, large stirring implements.

Magic Chant:
We're making witch stew,
We mix it up
We magic it up
We're making witch stew.

You find 1 bottle of water and put it in the pot;
We mix it once
We magic it once
We're making witch stew.

You find 2 stones and put them in the pot
We mix them twice
We magic them twice
We're making witch stew.

Etc.

Key Vocabulary: Next, add, more, number names.

Organisation: Small group

What to do: Tell the children that the worms in the garden are hungry and you have a special recipe called witch/wizard stew that is only fit for worms to eat! Explain that they will need to chant a special song and do some magic for the recipe to work. Show them the recipe and teach the magic chant, decide upon a magic action. The children find the ingredients and add them according to the recipe while chanting. When they have finished the worms can be fed. The cauldron and large mixing implements can be left for child initiated learning, but ensure that an adult is supervising what the children use in their recipes! Older children may like to record their own recipes.

Activity: Making Fruit Salad

Learning opportunity: Becoming aware of others likes and dislikes while working alongside them.

Early Learning Goal: Understand that people have different needs, views, cultures and beliefs that need to be treated with respect.

Resources: Variety of fresh fruit, knives, chopping boards, bowls, spoons, fruit juice

Key vocabulary: Please, thank you, like, dislike, more, some, less.

Organisation: Small group

What to do: Talk to the children about how good fruit is for their bodies, discuss what fruit they know, have tried and like and explain how mixed together it can be delicious. Discuss hygiene such as washing hands and then let the children choose a fruit to prepare into separate large bowls. When the bowls of separate fruit have been finished, they can wash their hands and then get a small bowl and choose what they want in their fruit salad. Encourage them to try fruits never tried before, make comments on how many pieces of fruit they have. You may want to say they can take no more than 5 pieces of the same fruit to encourage them to try more types. Older children can be challenged to record their salad choices maybe on a picture of a bowl and these fruit salad recipes can be made into a book. Younger children can take photos of their salads and later compare and count the fruit in the pictures.

Display

Make a display of photos of the children using recipes, cooking in play or for real, weighing and counting inside and outside. Add some questions such as ' who is weighing the carrots?' Add the favourite meal plates onto a table cloth in front. Make some laminated speech bubbles so that children can 'write' comments about the photos and adults can scribe their own and children's comments and tack them to the photos.

Week 4
Arty numbers

Personal, Social and Emotional Development
- Activity – make lift the flap books in a group. (PS1, 2, 7, 8)
- Show the children a picture of a planet far, far away, its called number planet but it is a sad place as there are no creatures living on it so you and the children need to create some number planet animals and people. Place a selection of resources with the dough- beads, cocktail sticks, feathers, shiny number sequins, bendy straws etc. Encourage them to use the resources independently to create creatures from Number planet. The children will probably think of other resources from the setting to use too. While you are all busy creating comment on how many tails, heads, feathers etc they are using, how could anyone know that the creature comes from the number planet? (PS1, 12)

Communication, Language and Literacy
- Reading the book *I spy 2 eyes* in small groups, finding the objects in the pictures, talk about and look at other books they know with numbers and pictures such as *One bear at Bedtime*. (L2, 3, 4)
- Set up a book-making table with plenty of resources for making their own 'I spy' books in child initiated learning time. Include magazines and catalogues for pictures as well as mark making materials. It is good practice for an adult to make their own book alongside the children, talking about the process as they do it. This helps children to organise their thinking. (L4, 10, 11, 12)

Problem Solving, Reasoning and Numeracy
- Read out a letter from Elmer saying that he would like a picnic blanket or duvet cover with lots of squares, all different colours. Give the children red, yellow and blue paint only and challenge them to make enough different colours to fill all the squares on a shaped piece of card, paper or material. Some children may like to work in pairs or a small group. When these are finished look at and count the different shades of blue for example. How many different blues/greens etc have they made? Older children could have more squares to fill in or they could design their own object for Elmer such as an umbrella or chair. (N1, 2)
- Hang bags containing 2D shapes on the washing line. Each bag has a number of same shapes in it. Working with a couple of children ask them to feel what is in their bag, guess the shape and number tip them out and count. When all bags have been emptied arrange the shapes into a picture on a board with a frame around it, take a photo of their art. These resources can be left available for other children to access independently. (N1, 2, 6, 11)

Knowledge and Understanding of the World
- Make some sticky number lines out of strips of card with double-sided tape attached. Take a group outside and look for natural objects to collect, remind the children about hygiene and safety issues. The children peal back the top layer from the tape when they have found something to stick on such as '1 leaf', '2 petals', '3 pieces of grass'. These number lines can be displayed together for comparison and discussion. (K1, 2, 9)
- Sit with one or two children and help them to use a computer-drawing programme to create pictures with numbers or numbers of objects. (K7)

Physical Development
- Collect pictures that include numbers from magazines, catalogues and clean food packaging. Children can be encouraged to cut out any numbers they can find and make a whole group collage that can be added to all week. When it is finished place a cardboard frame around it and hang it up for all to see. (PD7, 8)
- Make colour patterns with as many different resources as you and the children can find such as beads on strings, plastic recycled lids, construction bricks, crayons, plastic animals, vehicles, buttons, chalk on the ground outside… the list will be endless! While they are creating patterns talk about how many colours are being used, patterns you see in nature and on clothes. How many different patterns can they make with just 2 colours? Some of the patterns, such as those made on strings, can be hung together to make some modern art (have some modern art example to show them), other patterns that are made could

be photographed and displayed together, or made into a pattern book. (PD7, 8)

Creative Development
- Activity – creating large arty numbers. (C1, 3, 5)
- Make some plaster numbers by using florist's wire, plaster bandage wrap and plasticine. Prepare some lengths of wire and tape over the ends to ensure nothing is sharp. Look and feel and trace over with fingers 2D numbers made out of plastic or wood. Let the children experiment with the wire, making shapes and creatures and then numbers, place some part of the number into plasticine to hold it steady and then wet and wrap small pieces of plaster bandage around the wire, build up the layers to make chunky numbers, smooth over and leave to dry. The children can paint their model numbers however they like, leave to dry and then cover in PVA glue for a shiny tough finish. Remember that it doesn't matter if the numbers are not the perfect shape, what they are happy with you need to be happy with. These can be placed with the dough creatures on the numbers planet display. (C2, 3, 5)

Activity: Creating large arty numbers

Learning opportunity: Creating large pieces of artwork as part of a group.

Early Learning Goal: Explore colour, texture, shape, form and space in two or three dimensions.

Resources: Large cut out hardboard numbers, plastic sheeting, acrylic paint primary colours only, paint and ink type rollers, ride on vehicles, old clothing and outdoor space! Varnish.

Key Vocabulary: Mix, squeeze, squish, push, slide, roll.

Organisation: Small group for each hardboard number.

What to do: Place the number on some plastic sheeting, the children can squeeze or drop small amounts of paint onto the chosen number randomly, then cover with see through plastic sheeting and let them squash and push and roll the paint together, creating swirls and patterns and new colours, they can also ride over the number on their trikes or push small cars across. Observe and discuss when it looks good so that there are still different colours to see and different thickness of paint. Carefully peel off the plastic and leave to dry. They can be painted on both sides, varnished (adults only task) and placed in the outside area as a resource and artwork. Be aware that acrylic paint does not wash out of clothes easily so be careful when removing the plastic. The plastic will also be a work of art!!

Activity: Make group lift the flap books

Learning opportunity: To create a book as a group while learning about minibeasts and their habitat.

Early Learning Goal: Work as part of a group or class taking turns and sharing fairly.

Resources: A lift the flap book, paper, card, books about minibeasts and where they like to live.

Key Vocabulary: Under, beneath, behind, next to, inside.

Organisation: Small group

What to do: Look at a lift the flap book and books about minibeasts. Talk about their favourite minibeasts and where they are found such as under a stone, go for a walk in the outside area and see what they can find under and behind and beneath objects. Show the children how they can create a picture with a number of their chosen minibeast on one piece of card and then draw a stone or leaf on another piece of card to create a flap to make the animals feel safe. They can then make their own pictures and flaps, which can be made into a book, add questions to the pages such as 'can you guess what is under the leaf? How many animals are there?' The finished books can be placed in a basket with other books about minibeasts for the children to take outside in child initiated learning time.

Display
Hang up some starry dark material, place some 'terrain' in front, display the number planet creatures and plaster numbers for play and discussion.

Ensure all the art work created is displayed carefully and commented on by adults who enter the setting.

Week 5
Shopping with numbers

Personal, Social and Emotional Development
- Set up a shop in the role-play area with a small group of children, with price tags, a till and money. Sometime during the week pretend that some items have gone missing from the shop; discuss what this means and how they feel about it. Make a shopkeeper and a robber badge, the children can take turns to wear these and act out stealing from the shop, then they can talk about how they feel and how the shopkeeper feels what can be done to prevent this happening (a video surveillance camera) and what should happen to the robber. (PS4, 5, 9)
- In a small group play 'I went to the shop and I bought a …' memory game. With younger children have pictures or objects for them to choose and place in front of them to support their learning, older children can put pictures face down so they can be turned up if needed. (PS2, 3, 8)

Communication, Language and Literacy
- Read *The Great Pet Sale*. This can be at a time when all the children are together, if so ensure you give them time to talk together so that they are all involved in answers and thoughts about the book. Talk about how much each animal costs, what they would buy if they could only choose one, or only had 20p. Add up how much all the animals cost together by using pennies. Individual children can handle the pennies while all the children count. Trace over the animals from the story for the children to paint, these can be laminated and placed with the book for child initiated play. You may like to gather a collection of soft toys and place them in a box with a for sale notice on the outside. This can be left in the book area for the children to find and can initiate some wonderful shop play, writing for a reason, recording and writing of numbers. (L1, 2, 3, 4)
- Activity – make a story map. (L1, 4, 7, 13)

Problem Solving, Reasoning and Numeracy
- Activity – market day. (PD1, 2, 3, 4, 5)
- Play 'more or less' with a small group of children who have been using the vocabulary of more or less in their own games. Collect a variety of resources. Sit in a circle. Without the children seeing, put some objects in a bag, place a number of objects into the centre of the circle, choose one child to be the 'bag holder'- they must turn their back on the others. The other children and the adult pick a number card and collect that number of objects from the centre. Any leftover objects are cleared away. The bag holder turns back and counts out their objects, the other children call out more or less depending on the number they have compared to the bag holder. The bag holder chooses someone with more to be the next bag holder. (N1, 2, 3, 4, 6)

Knowledge and Understanding of the World
- Play alongside one or two children on a shopping game on the computer, such as *2simple Maths City 1* and *2*, where they need to pay with the correct money. (K7)
- Collect a treasure chest full of coins from around the world, allow the children to play, sort, match and count the coins, talk about the differences and the countries the coins come from. Play a lucky dip game where they close their eyes and choose a coin, show them how to make rubbings with paper and crayons, cut these paper coins out and place them on the correct countries on a map of the world. (K1, 3, 11)

Physical Development
- Print out some large and small pictures of English coins and notes and laminate them. Hang the large ones on the washing line and hide the smaller ones around the outside area. Look at and name the large ones with a small group of interested children, then tell them about the hidden small ones, they can go and find one piece of money at a time, bring it back to the line and peg it on the bigger version. The children will be zooming about so remind them to think about not bumping into others and also discuss why they are out of breath. (PD1, 2, 3, 4)
- A letter arrives from the small world people saying that they would like a market to do their

shopping in. Have a look at pictures of markets on Google images and in books. The children can help to plan and make market stalls and items to go on them. The children can then play with this resource in child initiated learning time. Once the market is made ensure the small world people write a thank you letter. (PD7, 8)

Creative Development

- Sing and act out five currant buns with pretend invisible food and coins. Make up different rhymes such as five ice-cream cones etc. Talk about how good it would be to have some currant buns, cones etc to use with the rhymes. Write a list of all the food from the rhymes and put it in the creative corner. (C4)
- Make some current buns out of salt dough, ice-cream cones from recycled material, etc in the creative area, ticking off the list as things are made. Practise the rhymes as items are made to make sure there are five of everything…or maybe change the rhyme to ten. These resources can be placed in a rhyme box with the rhyme typed out and a photo of the food on the top, the children can then borrow a box to take home and share the rhyme with their family. (C2, 3, 4, 5)

Activity: Market day

Learning opportunity: To add and subtract in purposeful play with others.

Early Learning Goal: In practical activities and discussion, begin to use vocabulary involved in adding and subtracting.

Resources: Resources from the setting plus sheets, tills, coins, bags, writing resources.

Key Vocabulary: How much, plus, subtract, change, more than, less than.

Organisation: As many children as want to be involved and plenty of adults and plenty of time!

What to do: Explain that you are going to set up a market in the outside area, look at some pictures and talk about markets the children have been to. The children can get into groups to set up different stalls, the need to think about the resources and then set their stall up, they will need to keep prices lower than 10p to make it easier. Once the stalls are ready the children and adults can take turns at being stall keepers and shoppers. As with all markets, when a certain time comes all the produce must be put away. Be prepared for market stalls being made in children's independent learning time following this session.

Activity: Make a story map

Learning Opportunity: To explore and re tell a story

Early Learning Goal: Retell narratives in the correct sequence, drawing on language patterns of stories.

Resources: Magazines, pictures from the computer (Google images), long roll of paper (wallpaper) sticky back plastic, a purse and some coins.

Key vocabulary: First, next, last.

Organisation: Small group.

What to do: Share the story 'My Granny went to market'. Discuss where she goes and what she buys. Explain that as she did lots of travelling you are going to make a story map to show her journey. Cut out or draw different parts of the story including the travel in-between counties. When you have the pictures they can be arranged on a long piece of stiff paper. Check nothing is missing and that it is in the correct order by reading the story again, stick the pictures on and cover in sticky back plastic. The children can then retell the story while walking along it, using coins to pay.

Display

Draw some shelves and stick on pictures of toys with price tags on to a display board, place similar toys on a table in front with blank tags for children to write on.

Week 6
We love numbers

Personal, Social and Emotional Development
- With the whole group talk about inviting friends and families to come and enjoy some number fun at the end of the week. Discuss what food and drink they would like to make over the week and who would like to make what. You will probably need a number limit for each item, so discuss this and make decisions together. Write up a shopping list of ingredients and a small group can go shopping. (PS4, 5)
- In small groups talk about all the different activities and games they have played over the last five weeks. Talk about what they liked doing best and choose some activities that they think their visitors may like to try. Write up their choices on a board; add to these when talking with other groups. Then ask all the children to vote for their favourite, look at the top three activities and help the children to organise the resources ready for the event. (PS2, 3, 4, 5)

Communication, Language and Literacy
- Activity – make invitations for the We Love Numbers Party. (L17, 18, 19)
- Talk about the food and drink they are going to make and help the children to write out/draw the simple recipes, and decorate them for the visitors to take away and try at home. Try to include some salad or vegetable sticks and dips. They will also need labels with the food so that their guests know what they can choose. (L17, 18, 19)

Problem Solving, Reasoning and Numeracy
- Look at the number line in the setting and talk about making a new one that includes all the children. The children can dress up as a certain character, such as a fireman and have their photo taken. Ensure that the children take the photos, look at them, and take another one if needed. Photos taken outside are generally better because of the light and background. Look at the photos together and put types together, two fireman, three angels etc. Where there are number gaps ask the children to dress up again as something you do not have. Print and laminate and then put in the correct order. This line could be displayed or can be used as a resource on the washing line or for games. (N1, 2, 3, 4)
- Make posters about numbers to put in the outside area, discuss how to cover them so that rain doesn't spoil them (PVA glue painted over the top/laminate). These posters may have lots of numbers on them or just one, allow the children the freedom to choose how they represent the numbers on their poster, help them to count and recognise numbers. Older children may be asked to do a more specific number poster, such as one showing addition or subtraction. (N3, 5)

Knowledge and Understanding of the World
- Make a whole group 'our favourite numbers' book. Using a simple drawing programme on the computer, each child can make a page about their favourite number, they can do a drawing of themselves with a speech bubble saying my favourite number is ___ because ___. Make sure all the adults in the room do their own page too and put them altogether to make a book. Maybe have a photo of the whole group on the front cover. (K7, 8)
- Those children who enjoyed the number hunt could be involved in designing an outdoor number hunt for the visitors, include the large numbers made in art week and natural resources. They will need to plan as a group, listen and discuss ideas, collect resources and make sure the hunt works by trying it out. (K6, 9, 10)

Physical Development
- Act out and sing some favourite action number rhymes, choose some to make props for and practise to show visitors when the come. The props may be masks, pretend food or simple puppets on sticks. Think about how to set up a stage area on the event day and discuss having tickets on pretend sale for performances. (PD1, 2, 4)

- Set up a 'duck pond' with a paddling pool and plastic ducks, add some duck size nets on sticks and some buckets. Using a timer see how many ducks they can catch and put in their bucket in a minute. Count and then try again. Vary and extend the game by putting numbers or spots on the ducks, can they catch all of a certain number or catch the ducks in the right order. Design a scoreboard for use in child initiated time and when the visitors come. (PD7, 8)

Creative Development
- Activity – make full size paper children with personal numbers. (C2)
- Make drinks and food as decided by the children in small groups, ensure they are aware of hygiene issues. Help the children to follow the recipes carefully and to think about how they are to store and present the food. (C1, 2)

Activity: Make full size paper children with personal numbers

Learning opportunity: To create a life-size picture of themselves while thinking about numbers that are important in their lives.

Early Learning Goal: Express and communicate their ideas, thoughts and feelings by using a widening range of materials and suitable tools.

Resources: Rolls of wallpaper, creative resources, number stamps and stencils, paint.

Key Vocabulary: Important, different, same, height, weight, number names.

Organisation: One or two children at a time.

What to do: Ask one child to lie down on the wallpaper, help the other to draw around them, and then swap over. The children can decide on paint or materials while the body outline is cut out (older children can cut out their own). They can decorate their body shape and then leave it to dry. When it is drying, or while they are decorating, they can think about numbers that are personal to them and the adult can scribe these onto shapes to be stuck on the body. Numbers such as their age, house number, number of siblings, pets, etc. These life-size bodies make a fantastic display and will promote lots of talk.

A collection of interesting objects, a roll of thick paper, mark making materials and some scissors placed together after an activity like this may be used by children in child initiated learning time, to help children consolidate skills and vocabulary.

Activity: Make invitations for the We Love Numbers Party

Learning opportunity: Writing for a real purpose and audience.

Early Learning Goal: Attempt writing for different purposes.

Resources: Examples of invitations, paper, card, mark making materials, envelopes.

Key Vocabulary: Date, time, day, invitation, reply.

Organisation: Small group.

What to do: Talk about who they would like to invite, friends and family. Look at a range of invitation cards and notice what they all have on them and how they are set out. Help the children to design a template on the computer and print it out for them to fill in with their own writing and decorate. (Many children will be writing in their own style so ensure that you have informed the parents of this event in plenty of time so that if they cannot read the invitation it does not matter. It is more important that the children are attempting to write for a real reason.) Each group will produce a different template, so make sure all the children are aware that the styles are different but the information is the same. Talk about the need for replies so that you can plan how much food and drink to make and maybe include a tear off strip. Place the invitation in an envelope that they can be encouraged to write on.

Letter writing materials should be made available in the writing or quiet area for child initiated learning time so that they can continue to practise writing for a reason.

Display
Make a display of the life-sized children pictures at child height so that they can find, compare and talk about the pictures and the numbers. Young children are very interested in themselves so it can promote questioning and discussion.

Bringing It All Together

Introducing the 'We Love Numbers Day'
- Discuss with the children how it would be a good idea to invite friends and family to join in with a number day. They can share some of the number activities they have enjoyed and show some of the work they have been doing.
- Encourage the children to think about some of the activities they have enjoyed during the previous weeks. Which do they think their families and friends would like to try?

Further Activity ideas
- Place some story sacks based on number stories on picnic blankets outside to share together.
- Place pictures of animals around the setting- inside and outside, give the guests a picture list to tally mark, can they find all the animals? Make a certificate for the person who finds the most.
- Small groups can entertain guests by acting out and singing number rhymes on a specially made stage. Place a rug on the floor and hang up a curtain and place some seats in rows in front of the area. You could 'sell' tickets for a performance, when there are ten tickets sold then a performance begins (have a pot of coins for the parents to access for this activity and encourage visitors to participate).

Involving children in preparation

Making refreshments
- Prepare fruit so guests can choose how many pieces to have in their fruit salad
- Make a number train cake – each carriage can have a different number on it, or number of candles, or form the shape of a number.
- Number shaped biscuits with icing and decorations.
- Currant buns with the five current buns rhyme by the plate.
- Make some fruit juice and allow the guests to choose three different flavours for their fruit cocktail.

Accessories
- Decorate a paper tablecloth with numbers; scatter some sequin numbers over the tablecloth around the plates of refreshment for a sparkly party look.
- Hang up balloons with numbers on around the setting and outside.

Resources

All books were available from leading booksellers at the time of writing

To collect/buy/make
- Florist's wire
- Plaster bandage
- Small coins, old coins, coins from other countries
- Pictures of markets
- Number cutters
- Hardboard
- Acrylic paint and rollers
- Animal Hats
- Gloves
- Velco spots
- Compost
- Large 'cauldron' like pots
- Double sided sticky tape
- Wallpaper rolls
- Shoeboxes

Everyday resources
- Magazines and catalogues
- Food packaging
- Recycled materials
- Odd socks, paired socks
- Percussion instruments
- Washing line
- Birthday cards
- Invitations

Stories/Non-fiction
- *Kippers Book of Numbers* by Mick Inkpen (Red Wagon Books)
- *One Smiling Sister* by Lucy Coates (Dorling Kindersley)
- *How Many Baby Pandas?* by Sandra Markle (Walker Books)
- *Bearobics* by Vic Parker (Viking Children's Books)
- *From the Garden* by Michael Dahl (Picture Window Books)
- Simple illustrated recipe books and cards
- *I Spy 2 Eyes* by Lucy Micklethwaite (Green Willow Books)
- *One Bear at Bedtime* by Mick Inkpen (Walker Books)
- Lift the flap books about minibeasts
- *The Great Pet Sale* by Mick Inkpen (Hodder Children's Books)
- *My Granny went to Market* by Stella Blackstone (Barefoot Books)

Songs and rhymes
(Print some out from the internet with illustrations and laminate for use indoors and outdoors)
- Number rhymes
- Number Songs
- Action rhymes
- *Makaton Nursery Rhymes Video* [VHS] Dave Benson 2001

Computer software/hardware
- Digital camera
- Dictaphone/recorder
- Electronic scales
- Electronic till
- Play phone/mobile
- 2Simple software *Maths City 1* and *Maths City 2*

Collecting Evidence of Children's Learning

Monitoring children's development is an important task. Keeping a record of children's achievements, interests and learning styles will help you to see progress and will draw attention to those who are having difficulties for some reason. If a child needs additional professional help, such as speech therapy, your records will provide valuable evidence.

Records should be the result of collaboration between group leaders, parents and carers. Parents should be made aware of your record keeping policies when their child joins your group. Show them the type of records you are keeping and make sure they understand that they have an opportunity to contribute. As a general rule, your records should form an open document. Any parent should have access to records relating to his or her child. Take regular opportunities to talk to parents about children's progress. If you have formal discussions regarding children about whom you have particular concerns, a dated record of the main points should be kept.

Keeping it manageable

Records should be helpful in informing group leaders, adult helpers and parents and always be for the benefit of the child. The golden rule is to make them simple, manageable and useful.

Observations will basically fall into three categories:
- **Spontaneous records:** Sometimes you will want to make a note of observations as they happen, for example, a child is heard counting cars accurately during a play activity, or is seen to play collaboratively for the first time.
- **Planned observations:** Sometimes you will plan to make observations of children's developing skills in their everyday activities. Using the learning opportunity identified for an activity will help you to make appropriate judgements about children's capabilities and to record them systematically.

To collect information:
- talk to children about their activities and listen to their responses;
- listen to children talking to each other;
- observe children's work such as early writing, drawings, paintings and 3D models. (Keeping photocopies or photographs is useful.)

Sometimes you may wish to set up 'one off' activities for the purposes of monitoring development. Some pre-school groups, for example, ask children to make a drawing of themselves at the beginning of each term to record their progressing skills in both co-ordination and observation. Do not attempt to make records after every activity!

- **Reflective observations:** It is useful to spend regular time reflecting on the children's progress. Aim to make some brief comments about each child every week.

Informing your planning

Collecting evidence about children's progress is time consuming and it is important that it is useful. When you are planning, use the information you have collected to help you to decide what learning opportunities you need to provide next for children. For example, a child who has poor pencil or brush control will benefit from more play with dough or construction toys to build the strength of hand muscles.

Example of recording chart

Name: Jamie Vaughan		D.O.B. 23.5.04		Date of entry: 13.9.09		
Term	Personal, Social and Emotional Development	Communication, Language and Literacy	Problem Solving, Reasoning and Numeracy	Knowledge and Understanding of the World	Physical Development	Creative Development
ONE	Plays alongside other children happily. Doesn't like help with dressing. 22.9.09 SJ	Enjoys stories with flaps and feely parts. Can make patterns in shaving foam, attempts letters for name. 11.12.09 PL	Likes to count, can rote count to 12, but needs help to count accurately above 5 objects. 16.11.09 SJ	Enjoys the computer, good control of mouse. 12.12.09 MB	Has good balance. Can build with large bricks. 24.10.09 PL	Enjoys playing with dough and clay, makes monsters by adding resources from the creative area. 6.10.09
TWO						
THREE						

Skills overview of six-week plan

Week	Topic Focus	Personal, Social and Emotional Development	Communication, Language and Literacy	Problem Solving, Reasoning and Numeracy	Knowledge and Understanding of the World	Physical Development	Creative Development
1	Number Hunt	Working and responding to others	Enjoying stories; Developing speech	Counting and recognising numbers	Investigate objects; Observe features in the environment	Move confidently and with control	Use a wide range of materials to create; Explore form in 3D
2	Musical Numbers	Be confident; Working with others	Exploring rhymes; Story elements	Solving practical number problems	Identify natural objects; Build and construct	Awareness of space and others	Creating sounds; Express and communicate ideas.
3	Cooking with Numbers	Understanding right and wrong; Using resources independently	Using language to discuss ideas and recreate stories	Comparative language; Mathematical vocabulary	Ask questions; Investigate with all the senses	Using tools and a range of equipment	Use imagination in design and creation
4	Arty Numbers	Forming good relationships; Considering consequences	Respond to stories; Experiment with writing.	Descriptive shape vocabulary	Use technology; Observation	Use tools and equipment safely	Explore colour, shape and texture in 2D and 3D
5	Shopping with Numbers	Work in a group; Confidence and interest	Developing vocabulary; Retelling	Using number names correctly in play	Use technology in play; Similarities and differences	Be aware of changes in their body when they run about	Sing songs from memory; Use imagination
6	We Love Numbers	Be aware of own needs and those of others	Writing for a purpose	Language for problem solving and comparison	Select and use tools; Think about their lives and others	Move with confidence; Use tools safely	Respond to their experiences and express their ideas

Home links

The theme of numbers lends itself to useful links with children's homes and families as there are many personal numbers related to children's home life. Through working together children and adults gain respect for each other and build comfortable and confident relationships.

Establishing Partnerships
- Keep parents informed about the topic of numbers and the themes for each week. By understanding the work of the group, parents will enjoy the involvement of contributing ideas, time and resources.
- Photocopy the parent's page for each child to take home.
- Invite friends, child minders and families to share all or part of the We Love Numbers event.

Visiting Enthusiasts
- The local shopkeeper could be invited to visit the setting's shop.
- Ask parents if they wish to be involved in the art week as extra help will be gratefully receive.

Resources requests
- Coins – old English coins or small change from holidays abroad
- Wallpaper rolls
- Shoeboxes
- Ask to borrow paint rollers
- Old invitations and birthday cards
- Simple recipes
- Favourite number rhymes

Preparing the event
It is always useful to have extra adults at events or when doing large scale art projects, and support in preparing food will be especially welcome.